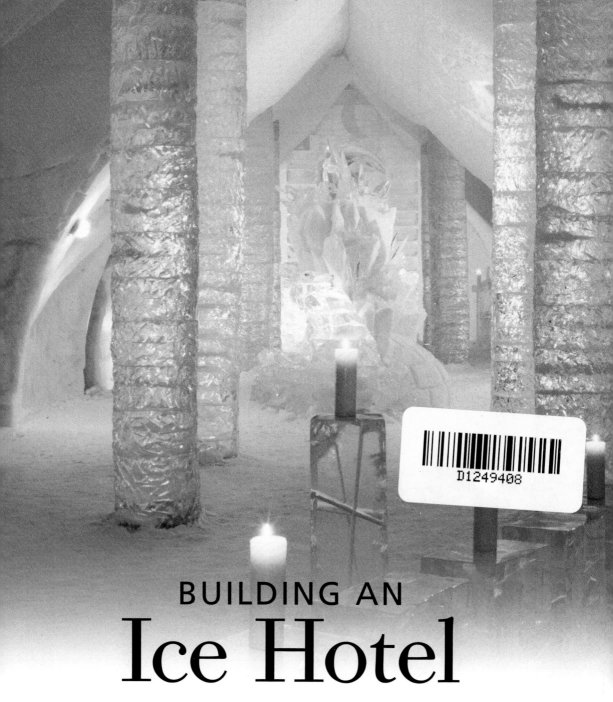

BUILDING AN
Ice Hotel

By Gib Goodfellow

D1249408

CELEBRATION PRESS
Pearson Learning Group

The following people from **Pearson Learning Group**
have contributed to the development of this product:

Joan Mazzeo, Dorothea Fox **Design** | **Editorial** Leslie Feierstone Barna, Teri Crawford Jones
Christine Fleming **Marketing** | **Publishing Operations** Jennifer Van Der Heide
Production Laura Benford-Sullivan
Content Area Consultants Dr. Amy Rabb-Liu and Dr. Charles Liu

The following people from **DK** have
contributed to the development of this product:

Art Director Rachael Foster

Martin Wilson **Managing Art Editor** | **Managing Editor** Marie Greenwood
Jane Tetzlaff **Design** | **Editorial** Hannah Wilson
Jo de Gray, Helen McFarland **Picture Research** | **Production** Gordana Simakovic
Richard Czapnik, Andy Smith **Cover Design** | **DTP** David McDonald
Consultant Jacques Desbois, CEO Ice Hotel Quebec-Canada Inc.

Dorling Kindersley would like to thank: Véronique Cyr and Marie-Noëlle Marceau at the Quebec Ice Hotel;
David Glover for additional consultancy; Rose Horridge in the DK Picture Library; Ed Merrit for cartography;
Kath Northam for additional design work; Mariana Sonnenburg for additional picture research; and Johnny Pau for additional cover design work.

Picture Credits: Alamy Images: Andre Jenny 10–11; Bryan and Cherry Alexander 4cl. Corbis: 23b; Nathan Benn 18bl; Perry Conway 26tc, 26tr,
26car; W. Geiersperger 8–9; Werner H. Müller 27tr; Anders Ryman 31tr; Randy M. Ury 26tl. Louis Ducharme: 1, 14–15, 17t, 20cr, 20–21.
Duchesnay Station Touristique: 7tr. Getty Images: Wayne R. Bilenduke 24tl; Andre Gallant 3; Steve Kaufman 30b; Sebastien Starr 24–25; Pete Turner
28–29. Ice Hotel Quebec-Canada: 4cl, 6–7, 8tr, 10tr, 12br, 12t, 14tl; Yves Tessier 16. Jan Jordan: 4–5, 16tr, 17bl, 19b, 30tl. Masterfile UK: Freeman
Patterson 21tr; Brian Sytnyk 25tr. National Geographic Image Collection: Roy Toft 27br. Rex Features: Norm Betts 13b, 19tr. Les Productions
Tessima Itée: Yves Tessier 21bl. Woodfall Wild Images: Tom Murphy 26bl. Cover: Louis Ducharme: front t. Ice Hotel Quebec-Canada:
front bl. Jan Jordan: back.

All other images: Dorling Kindersley © 2005. For further information see www.dkimages.com

ISBN: 0-7652-5236-8

Color reproduction by Colourscan, Singapore
Printed in the United States of America
6 7 8 9 10   08 07

1-800-321-3106
www.pearsonlearning.com

Contents

A World of Ice

Jacques Desbois (JAHK day-BWAH) has always loved winter. He loves the snow, the beauty of the woods, the excitement of winter sports, and building igloos— shelters made from blocks of snow. Jacques grew up in Quebec, a province of Canada where winter can last for many months and where Aboriginals have a long tradition of building igloos. Jacques' passion for snow led him to form a company that built igloos for festivals in Canada.

One day, Jacques learned about a hotel in Sweden that was made of ice and snow. It seemed like a strange idea— the guests sleep on beds of ice, and when the temperature rises in the spring, the hotel melts away! Yet to a man who built igloos for a living, the idea of building such a hotel was an exciting challenge.

Jacques Desbois is so expert in the construction of igloos and snow shelters that he is nicknamed "Mr. Igloo."

The Ice Hotel in Sweden was the inspiration for Quebec's Ice Hotel.

Jacques went to Sweden to meet with the hotel developers, and they explained to him how they had built their ice hotel. Jacques decided to try building his own in Quebec.

Back home were two Canadian businessmen looking for interesting new opportunities. They were excited by Jacques' project. The three men drew up plans and looked for additional investors. Meanwhile, Jacques also investigated different techniques that could be used for building the hotel.

Soon, several companies joined the project and provided equipment and money. Jacques and his partners borrowed money to buy more materials and more equipment, and to hire workers. Skilled workers came from Sweden to help train the people who would be building the hotel. At last, they were ready to start.

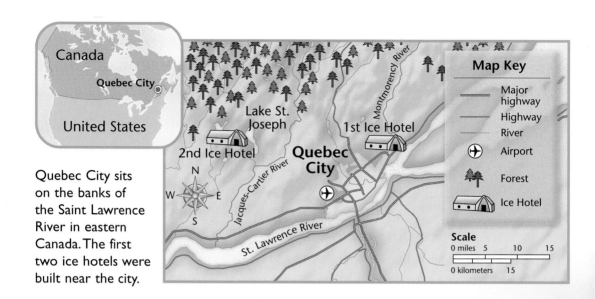

Map Key

▬▬▬	Major highway
────	Highway
⋯⋯⋯	River
✈	Airport
🌲	Forest
🏠	Ice Hotel

Labels on map: Canada, Quebec City, United States, Lake St. Joseph, 2nd Ice Hotel, Montmorency River, 1st Ice Hotel, Quebec City, Jacques-Cartier River, St. Lawrence River

Scale
0 miles 5 10 15
0 kilometers 15

Quebec City sits on the banks of the Saint Lawrence River in eastern Canada. The first two ice hotels were built near the city.

Jacques Desbois wanted to build the Ice Hotel close to Quebec City for three reasons. First, Quebec City has winters cold enough to keep an ice hotel frozen for several months. Second, Jacques and his partners lived there, and it would be easier for them to oversee the project. Third, Jacques knew he could find enough people in Quebec City to build and run the Ice Hotel.

In December 2000, Jacques built his first ice hotel, at Montmorency Falls, just northeast of Quebec City. It had space for twenty-two guests. The grand opening in January 2001 was covered by many newspapers and television stations. Guests came from all over the world to visit the Ice Hotel.

Jacques and his partners built a second hotel in the winter of 2002. This hotel was built in an area called the Duchesnay Ecotourism Station, northwest of Quebec City. Situated on more than 55 square miles of forest, the area has thirteen lakes. Guests were to stay one night in the Ice Hotel and other nights in the resort's cabins and lodges. They were to eat in the resort's restaurant and enjoy all the outdoor activities available at the site.

The cabins and lodges of the Duchesnay Ecotourism Station are located in the beautiful countryside that surrounds Quebec City.

Jacques and his team chose a site beside Lake Saint Joseph, the largest of the thirteen lakes. They needed a large, flat area and plenty of water to make snow. This site was perfect.

The water used to make the snow for the second Ice Hotel came from Lake Saint Joseph.

Building Begins

In July 2001, work started on the new Ice Hotel. Construction had to be completed in time for the opening planned for mid-January 2002. Architects designed the new Ice Hotel first. Then the engineers checked the plans to be sure that the building would be safe.

Workers at the building site followed the architects' plans closely.

Quebec can receive more than 30 inches of snow in December. In early December 2001, before much snow had fallen, the workers prepared the building site. Lumber and steel, which would be made into molds and frames for the walls of the Ice Hotel, arrived. Tractors and other heavy equipment for moving the building materials and the snow were brought to the site.

Why does water expand when it freezes?

Water is one of the only substances on Earth that expands when it freezes. This expansion occurs because the molecules move farther apart as the water reaches its freezing point (32 degrees Fahrenheit).

plastic bottle full of water

bottle bursts when water turns to ice and expands

Everything was ready to start, but there was not enough snow to make the hotel. There was little more than one month left to finish in time for the opening. The workers couldn't wait for nature to deliver snow. They had to make their own.

As soon as the temperature fell to 23 degrees Fahrenheit, water was pumped out of the freezing Lake Saint Joseph into three snow-making machines. These machines sprayed a fine mist that froze quickly in the cold air.

Snow-making machines create clouds of snow that are denser than natural snow. The machines spray water, which, if the air is cold enough, freezes to form snow.

The compacted snow that was created by the machines was perfect for building. In total, the builders needed to make more than 10,000 tons of compacted snow.

Jacques Desbois knew from his work with igloos and the first ice hotel, that snow was a wonderful building material. It was easy to move, very strong, and he could create beautiful shapes with it.

Snow-making machines created mounds of snow for the walls of the hotel.

Three forms of water: solid, liquid, and gas

Water is made up of tiny molecules. The way the molecules are arranged and move about depends on whether the water is in solid, liquid, or gas form.

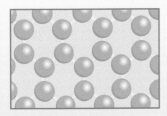

Ice (solid) molecules

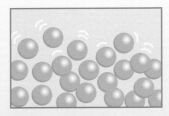

Water (liquid) molecules

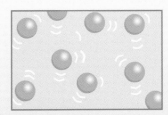

Water vapor (gas) molecules

Molecules in solids are arranged in a regular structure. Each molecule can vibrate but cannot move far. Solids, such as ice, have a fixed shape.

Molecules in liquids are not arranged in a regular structure. They can move about freely. Liquids, such as water, don't have a fixed shape.

Molecules in gases are more widely spaced than molecules in liquids. They move quickly and spread to fill the shape of their container.

Because of the trapped air between the snowflakes and within the snow crystals themselves, Jacques knew that the snow would act like a blanket to help insulate the building. Moving air carries heat away very quickly, but the tiny pockets of trapped air inside a layer of snow help block the flow of heat.

Most buildings have a frame of wood or steel onto which the walls and roof are attached. Building the Ice Hotel, however, was more like building with concrete. With concrete buildings, molds are used to keep the concrete in place until it hardens. Then the molds are removed.

The next step for the team was to make the molds that would determine the shape of the hotel. The molds would keep the snow in place until it hardened.

How do snowflakes form?

Snowflakes are a collection of tiny snow crystals. The crystals, such as those shown below, form when the water vapor in clouds freezes. The snow crystals may fall to the ground as they are, or they may stick together with other crystals to form large snowflakes. Snow crystals usually have six sides, and no two are exactly alike.

The molds were put in place
before being covered in snow.

The workers constructed metal
arches to act as the molds. The arches
had cross braces to support the
weight of the snow. Tractors moved
the steel molds into position. The
molds had ski-like runners along
their edges to allow them to be moved
more easily. Then snow was blown over
the molds to form ceilings and walls.
Finally, the snow had to freeze, which
took from ten to seventy-two hours.

The snow that covered the
molds froze to form ice.

After the snow hardened, everyone watched anxiously as the workers carefully removed the molds. When the last mold was removed, the team breathed a sigh of relief. The walls were strong and solid. They were more than 1½ feet thick at the highest point and twice as thick at the bottom. Jacques had used this design to make sure the base would be strong enough to support the weight of the ceiling. The plan had worked!

Workers added interior walls to divide the spaces into guest rooms. Then they removed the wooden frames that were used to create the doorways and hung curtains across the open spaces. Without real doors, there was no way to lock the guest rooms. Guests would have to leave their valuable belongings in another building.

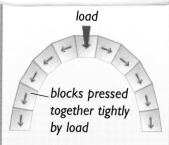

Why use arches?

load

blocks pressed together tightly by load

A flat roof is weak. The load in the middle makes it bend down, pulling the blocks apart at the joins. However, when the blocks are built up in a curved arch, the load squeezes them together more tightly. This makes the arch shape incredibly strong.

Finally, the molds were pulled out by tractors. They slid out easily on their ski-like runners.

Ice blocks came from Montreal. They were used for the construction of interior walls, pillars, and furniture.

Finally, all that was needed to complete the structure of the Ice Hotel was ice. Crystal-clear blocks of ice made from purified water were delivered to the site. Workers used the blocks to make walls at the ends of some sections of the hotel. These walls were strong and added to the beauty of the Ice Hotel.

The walls of ice were not just for decoration. They also let in natural light, which was important. Few electric lights were used because light bulbs produce heat, which would raise the temperature inside the hotel and cause the ice to melt. Still, every room was wired with electricity that passed along waterproof cables hidden in the walls, floors, and ceilings of the hotel.

The external structure of the Quebec Ice Hotel was finished. However, there was still much work to be done on the inside of the hotel before the guests arrived.

Finishing Touches

The structure of the Ice Hotel was complete, with sturdy walls and an elegant design. However, with no decorations, it seemed a little bare. It was time to decorate the interior.

Technicians started work on the Grand Hall first. The Grand Hall, with its 18-foot-high arched ceiling, would be the first room guests would see. Skilled workers made ice columns from blocks to help support the roof. These columns also added a decorative touch. Artists created ice sculptures and decorated the walls with carvings. Finally, the walls were polished to make them smooth and shiny. The Grand Hall was ready.

A chandelier made of ice hung in the Grand Hall. Light traveled along glass fibers inside the ice, reflecting light into the room but producing no heat.

This room is where food and drinks were served in the first Quebec Ice Hotel in 2001. For the 2002 hotel, this room had a slightly different, but equally beautiful, design.

Drinks were served in glasses made of ice.

Near the Grand Hall was a large room furnished with tables and chairs carved from ice and a long ice counter where drinks and food were served. Smoked meats and fish were served to guests on plates of ice. Even the glasses used to serve drinks were carved from ice. Of course, guests did not need ice cubes, but they probably needed gloves!

A theater near the Grand Hall had room to seat more than twenty guests. The films, which all had snow and ice as a theme, were projected onto a wall of pure white snow.

The Iroquois people made rattles from turtle shells. They filled the shells with pebbles and added a wooden handle.

The Ice Hotel also included two exhibition rooms, where guests could view artifacts of the Aboriginal peoples of Canada. Canada was home to the Iroquois, Algonquins, and Inuit long before European settlers arrived in North America. For the 2002 season, the exhibition was devoted to the Iroquois.

Before the hotel officially opened, the people of the Iroquois Nation arrived with historic artifacts for display. They decorated the exhibition room to look like the inside of their ancestors' wood and bark longhouses. First, they placed a frame of wooden poles inside the room. Next, they built beds along the walls. Then they made storage shelves above the beds. Finally, they hung corn, animal pelts, and tools from the wooden poles, just as their ancestors would have done. Although the walls of the exhibition were ice, and not bark, guests were able to get an idea of what it was like to live in a longhouse.

Up to twelve Iroquois families lived inside each longhouse. This is a reconstruction of a longhouse.

Cobs of maize were gathered in baskets and then hung to dry in the longhouses.

In the second exhibition room were ice sculptures, including those of two herons, a salmon, and a statue honoring Hector de Saint-Denys Garneau, one of the greatest poets of Quebec. Ice for these sculptures had to be specially made from purified water to ensure that it was crystal clear to reflect the light.

A sculptor at the Ice Hotel used a chainsaw to carve an ice model of an Inuit inside an igloo.

Magnificent ice thrones were sculpted for the hotel.

In every guest room was an ice bed. Ice slabs with lights formed the bases of the beds. Wooden boxes set on the bases kept the guests comfortably off the ice. A foam cushion and deerskins covered the boxes. Guests were also given warm sleeping bags and pillows.

A bathroom trailer was connected to the hallway. The trailer contained a toilet, a sink, and, happily for the guests, an electric heater. Guests could prepare for bed and get dressed in the morning in comfort.

Fireplaces added a cheerful glow to some guest rooms. They were specially designed not to produce heat, which would melt the walls.

The heated trailer was the warmest place in the hotel. Everywhere else the temperature was between 23 and 28 degrees Fahrenheit. That's just below the temperature at which water freezes (32 degrees Fahrenheit).

Outside the hotel were grounds where people could meet to enjoy bonfires and fireworks. There were also hot tubs for soaking and splashing. Next to the tubs were mounds of fresh snow. Brave guests could take a "snow bath" by rolling in the snow before jumping into the hot tubs.

Why does ice look blue?

Light is made up of photons, or light particles. Photons with different amounts of energy have different colors. Red and orange photons have less energy than blue photons. Pure ice is almost completely transparent. Most photons travel right through it. However, a few of the photons give up their energy and are absorbed by ice molecules. More red and orange photons are absorbed than blue, so the remaining light has a blue tint. This is why ice looks blue when it transmits or reflects light.

The guests at the Ice Hotel were treated to fireworks displays at night.

Exploring a Frozen World

The Ice Hotel was completed on time, and the first guests arrived on January 15, 2002. During the day, the guests were busy outdoors. There was so much to do. Guests could go hiking, cross-country skiing, or ice skating. They could whiz about on dogsleds or snowmobiles. They could go ice fishing or learn the history of the fur trade. They could also learn about the wildlife in the forests around them.

Ice skating was popular. Jacques had included an unusual skating rink that was half indoors and half outdoors. Guests could glide about in the sparkling sunshine, and then skate back inside to the snack bar for a cup of hot chocolate!

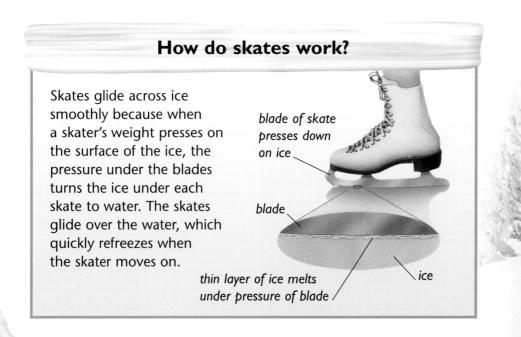

How do skates work?

Skates glide across ice smoothly because when a skater's weight presses on the surface of the ice, the pressure under the blades turns the ice under each skate to water. The skates glide over the water, which quickly refreezes when the skater moves on.

blade of skate presses down on ice

blade

thin layer of ice melts under pressure of blade

ice

Guests who chose to hike found that the snow around the Ice Hotel was packed down neatly. In the woods, however, the snow was nearly 2 feet deep, so guests had to lift their feet high enough to walk. Many people wore snowshoes, which kept them on top of the snow and made walking more comfortable. The guests followed a trail that covered more than 6 miles around the Ice Hotel.

During the 2002 season, the most popular activity at the hotel was cross-country skiing. Guests skied on more than 90 miles of trails. They stopped at heated huts along the ski trails to rest and have a hot drink.

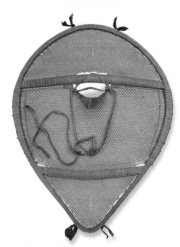

Aboriginal snowshoes consist of netting attached to frames. The wide, flat design helps spread weight evenly, so that feet do not sink into the snow.

⓵ Winter sports can be dangerous. Never ski or hike outdoors without an experienced guide.

Guests could also try ice fishing from heated fishing shacks on the frozen lake. Guests sat in the shacks and put their fishing lines into the water through holes cut in the ice. They chatted and relaxed while they waited for the fish to take the bait.

Other guests explored the far corners of the resort area by dogsled. A musher, who cared for the dogs and the sleds, met the guests at the hotel.

Inuit people sometimes use harpoons to fish. Guests at the Ice Hotel used an easier method—fishing lines.

Two or three people sat on the sled beneath deerskins, which kept them warm. The musher ran behind the sled and jumped on when the dogs ran faster. He called out directions to the lead dog, who turned left or right on command.

Another popular activity at the Ice Hotel was snowmobiling. Guests sped along the trails on frozen Lake Saint Joseph. They wore special snowmobile suits to keep them warm and helmets with windshields to protect their faces from the cold and wet.

Huskies are excellent sled dogs. They have thick, warm fur and can move quickly over great distances.

Many guests enjoyed snowmobiling, but the noise of the vehicles scared away wildlife.

25

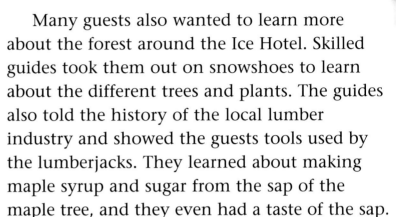

Snow preserves a record of recent animal movement.

Guests at the hotel learned how sap is collected from maple trees to make syrup.

Many guests also wanted to learn more about the forest around the Ice Hotel. Skilled guides took them out on snowshoes to learn about the different trees and plants. The guides also told the history of the local lumber industry and showed the guests tools used by the lumberjacks. They learned about making maple syrup and sugar from the sap of the maple tree, and they even had a taste of the sap.

Guests who were interested in Canadian history could learn about fur trappers of the past. A guide, wearing the clothing of the historic fur traders of Quebec, taught guests how trappers stretched hides on wooden frames and transported furs by canoe.

The red fox can adapt to habitats as different as city parks and the snow and ice of the Arctic.

Guests were able to try the traditional foods of the fur trader. These included bannock (bread made over an open fire) and pemmican (dried meat and peas).

Some guests chose to learn about wildlife in the forest. Fur was found where a moose had scratched its hide on a tree. Piles of feathers showed that a hawk had just had dinner. Deer and moose were occasionally seen, but often the smaller animals, such as mink and weasel, left only their footprints in the snow.

At night, there was an owl outing. First, a guide told about the great gray owl, which is common in the surrounding forest. Then the guide led the guests out into the snowy woods. Everyone was silent as they listened for the owl's cry.

The great gray owl can plunge into snow to catch its prey.

The moose is the largest member of the deer family.

The Season Ends

At the end of March, the hotel staff said goodbye to the last guests and prepared to close the Ice Hotel. So much hard work had gone into making and running the hotel, but in a few days, it would be just a memory. Supplies such as the deerskins, bed boards, lights, and wires were removed and put in storage for next year. The bathroom trailer was towed away.

When only ice and snow remained, the hotel was ready for destruction. It might have been fun to watch it slowly melt. However, the danger of someone entering the structure and getting hurt was too great, so the work had to be done quickly.

Workers drove huge machines over the top of the Ice Hotel. In only five hours, the machines destroyed what had taken five weeks to build. The Ice Hotel was gone, with the ice and snow that had been used to construct it now part of the wintry Quebec landscape.

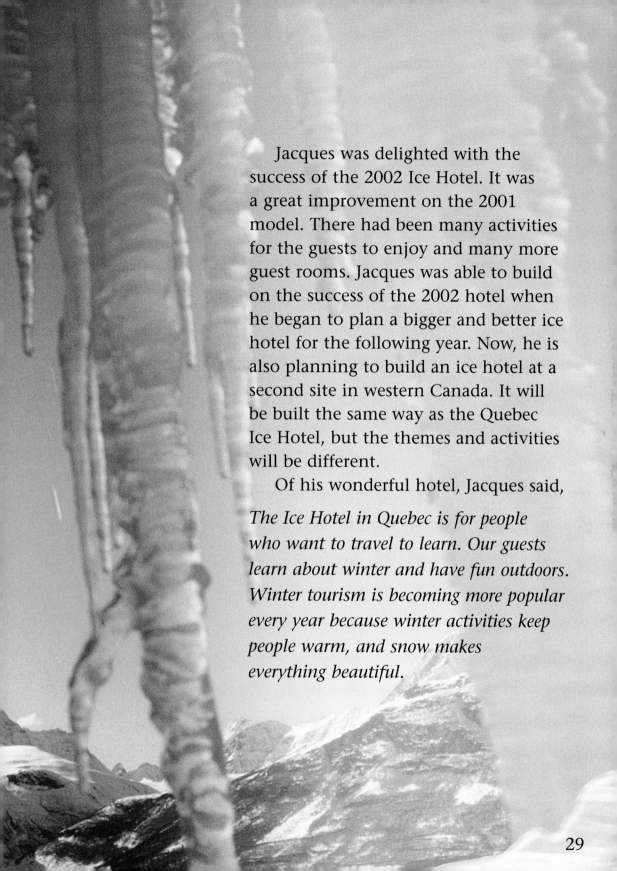

Jacques was delighted with the success of the 2002 Ice Hotel. It was a great improvement on the 2001 model. There had been many activities for the guests to enjoy and many more guest rooms. Jacques was able to build on the success of the 2002 hotel when he began to plan a bigger and better ice hotel for the following year. Now, he is also planning to build an ice hotel at a second site in western Canada. It will be built the same way as the Quebec Ice Hotel, but the themes and activities will be different.

Of his wonderful hotel, Jacques said,

The Ice Hotel in Quebec is for people who want to travel to learn. Our guests learn about winter and have fun outdoors. Winter tourism is becoming more popular every year because winter activities keep people warm, and snow makes everything beautiful.

Ice Adventures Around the World

Today, there are ice hotels in other countries besides Canada and Sweden. In Greenland, the Igloo Village Hotel is a collection of igloo-like domes of snow that are connected by snow passageways and lit by candles. Finland also has an Igloo Village in Kakslauttanen (kak-slow-TAH-nen). Guests can visit a reindeer farm and learn about the Saami, the native people of Scandinavia.

Hotels are not the only places where snow and ice are celebrated. A festival in Sapporo, Japan, is dedicated to ice and snow. Every February, the city is transformed with ice sculptures and structures. There are huge carvings of gods and goddesses, palaces, and even the pyramids of Egypt.

A fishing trip in a boat made of ice is one adventure visitors to Sweden won't forget!

Visitors to Japan's Snow and Ice Festival enjoy an ice slide.

In northern Sweden, there is a two-story theater made of snow and ice. At night, spectators sit on reindeer skins, which cover the icy seats, to watch performances by Saami actors. During the intermission, the spectators can have a warm drink and gaze up at the stars above, as the theater has no roof. Every springtime, the theater melts, but every winter it is rebuilt for another season.

These Saami actors are performing on a stage made of ice.

Snow and ice are not only enjoyed in cold countries. Ice sculptors create magnificent ice sculptures for displays in hotels and restaurants in many parts of the world, not just the Ice Hotel in Canada. All an ice sculptor needs is a large refrigerator to stop the sculpture melting before it goes on display!

Matsumura, an ice sculptor from Japan, carves a swan for a hotel display.

Index